SIDES OF GRIEF

DIEGO MESA

This book does not replace the advice of a medical or mental health professional. Consult your physician before making any changes to your diet or regular health plan.

SIDES OF GRIEF
ISBN: 978-1-7378702-8-9
Copyright© 2025 by Diego Mesa
www.PATRIA.church

Printed in the United States of America. All rights reserved. This book or portions thereof may not be reproduced in any form without the prior written permission of the copyright owner. The only exception is brief quotations.

Unless otherwise noted, Scripture is taken from the New King James Version® (NKJV). Copyright © 1982 by Thomas Nelson. Used by permission. All rights reserved.

Scripture quotations marked (NLT) are taken from the Holy Bible, New Living Translation, copyright © 1996, 2004, 2007, 2013, 2015 by Tyndale House Foundation. Used by permission of Tyndale House Publishers, Inc., Carol Stream, Illinois 60188. All rights reserved.

Scripture quotations marked AMP are taken from the Amplified Bible. Copyright © 1954, 1958, 1962, 1964, 1965, 1987 by The Lockman Foundation, La Habra, CA. Used by Permission. All rights reserved.

Scripture quotations marked NIV are taken from the Holy Bible, New International Version®. NIV® Copyright© 1973, 1978, 1984, 2011 by Biblica, Inc. All rights reserved.

Scripture quotations marked ERV are taken from the Holy Bible, Easy-to-Read Version. Copyright© 2001 by the World Bible Translation Center. Used by permission. All rights reserved.

All Scripture quotations are taken from THE MESSAGE, copyright © 1993, 2002, 2018 by Eugene H. Peterson. Used by permission of NavPress. All rights reserved. Represented by Tyndale House Publishers, Inc.

CONTENTS

Introduction | 1

Dimensions of Grief | 7

Change and Reaction | 15

Influence and Focus | 29

Cycles and Setbacks | 39

Jesus' Acquaintance with Grief | 53

A New Normal | 59

The Greater Gain | 65

Prayer and Inspirational Verses | 77

White Gladioli symbolize purity and spirituality.
The flowers that precede each chapter in this book are familiar offerings of endearment meant to console those who experience a loss.

INTRODUCTION

When I was a young boy, there was a bully in my neighborhood named Kenny who scared the life out of me. To me, he was like a miniature King Kong. He was huge, mean, and intimidating. Kenny was initially my friend, but at some point, he changed. He began to make every day of my life miserable. He pushed me around, took my things, and threatened to knock my block off (punch me), which he did a few times.

One day, after several encounters with Kenny, I asked my dad to teach me how to box. I wanted to learn to defend myself against Kenny and others like him. It took several months for me to develop the skills and courage, but I was determined because I was fed up with the grief and misery.

Eventually, the day arrived. It was time to put into practice what I learned. I stood before Kenny, full of fear and with eyes welling up with tears. I told Kenny, "I won't be pushed around anymore." I stood my ground and was ready to fight to be free from his affliction. Kenny looked at me, and realizing I was serious about not allowing him to continue to disrupt my life, he waved me off and walked away. From that day forward, Kenny never bullied me again.

Romans 8:37-39 (NIV) is a fitting verse to confess in situations like mine. It reads as follows:

> ...In all these things we are more than conquerors through Him who loved us. For I am convinced that neither death nor life, neither angels nor demons, neither the present nor the future, nor any powers, neither height nor depth, nor anything else in all creation [including grief], will be able to separate us from the love of God that is in Christ Jesus our Lord.

Notice that the words "neither" and "nor" are stated ten times by the Apostle Paul. The repeated use of these words is meant to emphasize or draw attention to something important, and that is nothing we experience, neither in death nor in life, can separate (divide, disconnect, distance) a believer from the love of God. That would include grief.

Grief (sorrow, mourning, despondency, anguish) is experienced in various scenarios, but the reason behind grief is generally the same. It's the result of an experienced loss or distress. What tops the list of things for which people experience grief is the loss of a relationship. That can include a loved one, a marriage, or another type of bond.

In addition to grieving the loss of a relationship, some grieve the loss of a job, career, or retirement plan. Some grieve the loss of a home. Some grieve the way their body used to look. Some grieve dreams that never materialized or the peace and happiness they used to have.

The loss of people (spouse, child, parent, sibling, extended family, friends), which is the primary focus of this book, tends to be the greatest heaviness experienced in life. Unexpected deaths can be the most difficult. Even when death is expected, it doesn't always make grief easier to deal with. It's yucky! Or, if you permit me to say, It sucks!

The Bible reveals that grief is a part of life. It also speaks of our mortality and immortality, which means that every person will have an eternal existence after our physical existence ends.

> "Then shall the dust return to the earth as it was: and the spirit shall return unto God who gave it."
> —Ecclesiastes 12:7 (KJV)

There is an old African saying that speaks of the loss of a loved one. It declares that when a loved one dies, they haven't departed; they have arrived.

Nan Witcomb has this to say about loss:

> We do not have to rely on memories to recapture the spirit of those we have loved and lost – they live within our souls in some perfect sanctuary which even death cannot destroy.

NO MORE TEARS

When you hear the phrase "No More Tears," do you connect it with a slogan for baby shampoo? If so, you're not alone. In 1953, Johnson & Johnson Baby Shampoo's debut was promoted as a very mild shampoo perfect for a baby's sensitive skin. The "No More Tears" promotion suggested that even if some shampoo got into a child's eyes during bath time, it was so gentle it wouldn't hurt.

The product won the hearts of millions, eliminating the daily drama experienced during bath time for babies and parents, which was painful, frustrating, and caused fear. Could this scenario have a broader meaning or application for us today?

In 2005, a documentary was produced to chronicle the lives of eight children who survived the December 2004 Indian Ocean earthquake and tsunami (also known as the Boxing Day Tsunami) that occurred off the west coast of northern Sumatra, Indonesia. The earthquake registered a magnitude of 9.1 to 9.3 and produced a series of tsunami waves up to 100 feet high. As a result, an estimated 227,898 people in 14 countries lost their lives. It was devastating and heartbreaking.

The documentary was titled *Children of Tsunami: No More Tears*. It depicts the aftermath and horrific suffering, sorrow, and grief experienced by the children and their families who lost loved ones, homes, personal possessions, and their livelihoods. It details the challenges they faced during their journey to rebuild their shattered lives. The amazing story is a true testament to the human spirit's determined will to live on after tragedy. "Is that possible," you ask. The answer is yes, it is possible.

"The end of a matter is better than its beginning…"
—Ecclesiastes 7:8 (NIV)

This verse in Ecclesiastes speaks of a great promise, right?

INTRODUCTION

Many tears are shed, much crying is experienced, and deep sorrow is felt when someone dies. There is an overwhelming void in the core of one's being, and an emptiness exists when someone suffers the loss of a loved one. People can enter a season where they feel they're not themselves because they have never been where the loss has taken them. The full spectrum of emotions can be experienced during that season.

> "I'm not sure which pain is worse—the shock of what happened or the ache for what never will."
> —Author Unknown

Fortunately, we have a Creator and Savior, Jesus, who understands the depth of our souls' aches and the anguish we suffer during unhappy and unwanted seasons. He is the one who designed us with the ability to release tears of sadness, tears of love, tears of anger, tears of loneliness, and tears of regret.

1 Peter 5:7 encourages us to cast our cares (all those tears) upon Jesus, which means to look toward Him and allow Him to cry with us. It means we give our sorrow to Him. Why? Because we sometimes feel broken and need to be fixed. We feel damaged and need to be restored. We feel helpless and need hope.

Realize that Jesus wept like you and weeps with you. Jesus understands the emotions you're experiencing. They are very precious to Jesus. Jesus understands that weeping can feel like it will never end, but it does have an ending. I promise you.

Psalm 147:3 tells us, "He heals the brokenhearted." Psalm 30:5 states, "Weeping may last for the night, but rejoicing comes in the morning," and according to Psalm 56:8, our tears are collected in a bottle.

White Carnations symbolize innocence, youth, and purity.

CHAPTER 1

DIMENSIONS OF GRIEF

Grief is like a multifaceted diamond with many angles. For some, grief feels like living in the aftermath of a terrible wreck. It may feel like a TKO (technical knockout)—the powerful, stunning blow of a boxer's punch. Some may experience an overwhelming sinking feeling like that felt by those aboard the Titanic—that going down or drowning feeling. It may feel like a bad dream one cannot wake up from. It may feel like a dense cloud that rolls in and impedes one's ability to see or think clearly. No matter the feeling, it is pretty real and raw.

For some, grief is not expressed in tears, and may I state that not crying is not wrong, just like crying is not wrong. Not crying does not mean someone feels less sadness over a loss. It does not mean the person does not care or is denying reality. Tears may or may not come, but the expression of grief does manifest, and it's natural, expected, and understandable.

Some cannot go to work for a while after a loss, and work isn't a challenge for others. Some question the loss of a loved one, and others don't question it at all. Some need counseling, and others can process their grief without assistance. For some, the effects of the event are temporary, and for others, they are permanent. At the end of the day, every one of us is wired differently (a personality bent), so we react differently. There are some things we cannot chart with graphs, steps, levels, and stages. We are all made wonderfully and uniquely different.

Not often is anyone simply okay with death; it is not comfortable or easy. There is never a good or right time to die. Many times, we can feel like we are strong and doing well with grief, only to have something trigger our emotions, and those uneasy feelings surface.

A trigger can be a smell, song, place, date, or memory, and it can come upon us like an unseen pothole or speed bump in the street. It's unsettling and may slow your forward progress. It may make you feel like you are riding the ocean's tide and being pulled backward. It may make you feel like a yo-yo or a seesaw with up and down cycles. Whatever the feelings, I encourage you not to allow them to stop you from moving forward.

To grieve when we experience loss is expected. It is important to know that there is a good process for grief. What do I mean by that? Good sadness or good grief is when a person can recover emotionally within a healthy period as opposed to finding it difficult to recover from a loss.

When someone experiences loss, generally, a series of reactions naturally occur as the individual processes the loss. The initial reactions are shock and denial. Most cannot believe what has happened. Some become numb to the situation and don't know how to move past it. They tell themselves, "This is not happening;

this cannot be real." It's as if they had the wind knocked out of them, leaving them dazed and confused. Denial may keep some from willingly talking about or accepting it.

Once reality sets in, individuals may feel like they are on an emotional roller coaster. They are not sure how to react. They may feel angry, guilty, depressed, rejected, lonely, abandoned, or regretful. Realize there is no right or wrong order for these emotions.

Some may ask why or wonder if they could have done more. Some may state, "This isn't fair or right," or they simply try to cope with the circumstances. This is all predictable and understandable.

> "I thought I could describe a state; make a map of sorrow. Sorrow, however, turns out to be not a state but a process."
> —C.S. Lewis.

In the quote by C.S. Lewis, he uses the word "process" to summarize grief. Perhaps another word to consider is journey as the passage of time leads many to full recovery.

Generally, the final phases of grief are acceptance and recovery, and here is where a lot of people fall short. It's understood that grief is difficult, but when someone lingers in it instead of recovering from it, their mourning can turn into feelings of hopelessness. Hopelessness is a dangerous emotional state that should be avoided or at least resisted. Unfortunately, giving up and not moving forward is a decision some make.

People can react in destructive ways because of hopelessness and turn to things they shouldn't to escape or hide the pain. There are those who have attempted to mask the pain with emotional outbursts and damaging actions. Some choose sex, rage, isolation, and other adverse behavior, including suicide to escape. Some choose an insensible lifestyle of abuse, misuse, and neglect. They seem to no longer care about things that used to matter or were important to them.

A silent condition that some people use like a comfortable blanket is loneliness. It is becoming an epidemic as a result of the fragile state of people and society. Loneliness occurs when there is an interruption in life. The interruption creates gaps that are not being filled. Sometimes, dependence on the state of the world and the lack of personal identity and purpose make people lonely. Loneliness can lead to discomfort and distress.

Dr. Vivek Murthy vs. Surgeon General states, "One in two adults in America struggles with loneliness." It also states, "Loneliness is an epidemic in America." In 2021, because of COVID-19, Japan appointed a Minister of Loneliness to try and solve the issue in its country.

The Bible states in Ecclesiastes 3:1, 4, "To everything there is a season, a time for every purpose under heaven…A time to weep, and a time to laugh; a time to mourn, and a time to dance."

The Bible contains several examples that describe periods of mourning, including Jacob's death (70 days), Moses' death (30 days), and Aaron's death (30 days). The takeaway from these examples is that there was a period of mourning, which means there was, so to speak, an expiration or termination date.

God's love is unfailing, and He doesn't want us to lose hope during our time of mourning. His Word says in 1 Thessalonians 4:13, "But I do not want you to be ignorant, brethren, concerning those who have fallen asleep [the dead], lest you sorrow as others who have no hope." In other words, we should not grieve like those who don't know what their future holds, or what's next after death.

As believers, we are on a different course in life. Our weapons or prescriptions are different from that of the unsaved. Yes, we do grieve, but our recovery process is completely different from those who do not know God. Here is a truth: The only way to go to Heaven and be with Jesus is the doorway of death. We are resurrection people.

To grieve for a moment is expected; however, after sufficient time has passed, we are to gain a proper perspective and understanding, and take hold of the truth and promise so that healing can take place. There still may be moments of sadness, darkness, or depression, and that is okay, but they are moments. Moments are short-term, not long-lasting.

Time changes everything and time can heal. Let me explain. If we were to experience a hurricane today, there would be little to no evidence of the devastation that occurred in a year or two from now because nearly everything would be restored.

In the same way, when we look at pictures of past wars—World War I, World War II, the Korean War, and the Vietnam War—it's apparent that countries, cities, and neighborhoods directly impacted were left decimated (bombed, burned, and buried). Although mass devastation occurred in various locations in the early 1900s, '40s, '50s, and '60s, if we were to visit them today, there would be little to no sign of what took place so long ago.

The cities have been completely restored. As a matter of fact, I took a trip a couple of years ago to Germany, and I couldn't believe how beautiful some of the areas were that had previously been ravished by war.

So it is in God. There is life after death, restoration after loss, and God can redeem the pain with a purpose.

How does one find the path to good grief? First, it is important to understand that grief is a very personal and sensitive situation.

As a pastor, I have consoled thousands of people, and I have found that when individuals experience loss, they seem to go through the process more at ease when they feel the presence of peace in their lives. That is when someone is able to feel comfort rather than confusion, and when one can grasp the promise instead of the problems. It is being eternity focused rather than focused on this physical world. That is when grief becomes lighter. I am not saying the process is easy but it is also not as weighty or insurmountable.

Arthur Henry Kenney, an Irish priest and Dean of Achonry at the Church of Ireland from 1812 to 1821, stated the following:

> Thanks be to God – that believers do not have to grieve like the world who have no real hope. I really believe if, instead of shutting ourselves into our sorrows and keeping all the light of heaven out of our souls, we opened them to receive Him, Christ would so come to us that the season of our deepest grief and anguish would become one of the richest and most precious of our whole lives.

If you are presently experiencing grief, please know that peace is available to you by simply inviting Jesus, the Prince of Peace, into your circumstances. No matter how great the sadness is in your life, it does not have to last. God is faithful to rebuild and restore your life after a loss.

Joel 2:25 states, "So I will restore to you the years that the swarming locust has eaten, The crawling locust, The consuming locust, And the chewing locust, My great army which I sent among you." This verse encourages us to understand that God can heal us and restore the lost years that have been devoured by the swarming, crawling and consuming locust that have raided our lives.

No matter the depth of your loss, be reminded that God is able to restore you with hope, genuine strength, and courage to move forward in your faith and life. The season you are in may have caught you off guard, but it did not catch Him off guard. He saw the day you suffered the loss. He saw you, and He knows what you are feeling and where you are in your healing process, and He has made provision for you. His grace (supernatural strength to succeed) is sufficient for everything that you are experiencing. You may want to repeat that to yourself and allow it to sink in.

> "In times of grief and sorrow, I will hold you and rock you and take your grief and make it my own. When you cry, I cry, and when you hurt, I hurt. And together, we will try to hold back the floods to tears and despair and make it through the potholed street of life."
> —Nicholas Sparky

White Orchids symbolize reverence, innocence, and purity.

CHAPTER 2

CHANGE AND REACTION

In biblical times, sackcloth, a fabric usually made of black goat hair, was used to make a covering or coat. It had a strong odor, and it was not comfortable to wear. It was customary for people to wear sackcloth as a sign of mourning.

When Joseph was sold into slavery by his brothers, they went home and told their father Jacob that Joseph had been killed. Because of his grief, Jacob put on sackcloth and went into mourning (Genesis 37:34).

The Bible tells about Nineveh repenting when Jonah came to them, and they put on sackcloth as a sign of repentance (Jonah 3:5-8).

When Mordecai heard of the edict that the king signed to annihilate the Jewish people, he put on sackcloth and went into mourning (Esther 4:1).

The Bible reveals to us that it is okay to grieve. There was an appropriate season when garments were worn to mourn, but at some point, the mourning attire had to be removed. Unfortunately, many continue to struggle with releasing their mourning garments (figuratively). They go to the gym, work, the mall, and on vacations dressed in their mourning garments of sadness, weightiness, and uncomfortableness.

We read in 2 Samuel 12 how King David experienced grief after the loss of his infant son. The verse describes David's state after hearing about the loss.

> Then David got up from the ground. After he had washed, put on lotions and changed his clothes, he went into the house of the LORD and worshiped. Then he went to his own house, and at his request they served him food and he ate.
> —2 Samuel 12:20 (NIV)

Notice David's reaction: He changed his clothes—took off the sackcloth that he was likely wearing—took a bath, and went to the house of the Lord to worship. After he worshiped, he went to his house and requested food. He probably had not eaten much in days because his child was gravely ill.

David asked for food to be served, and his servants questioned him (2 Samuel 12:21), "Why are you acting this way? While the child was alive, you fasted and wept, but now that the child is dead, you get up and eat!"

The servants were essentially telling David that he was doing the opposite of what most would do under those circumstances. A time of mourning was expected after the child's death, yet David reacted differently.

David answered his servants. According to 2 Samuel 12:22-24 (NIV), this was his response:

> While the child was still alive, I fasted and wept. I thought, 'Who knows? The Lord may be gracious to me and let the child live.' But now that he is dead, why should I go on fasting? Can I bring him back again? I will go to him, but he will not return to me.
>
> Then David comforted his wife Bathsheba, and he went to her and made love to her. She gave birth to a son, and they named him Solomon.

I want to focus on a few key points in this story as it relates to grief. First, David was at a place of sorrow, but he did not stay there. He changed his clothes and put his mourning wear (unattractive, black, dark) back on the rack. We know that David did not stay there because the Bible tells us that he washed himself, anointed himself, and changed his clothes. He removed himself from the place of grief and began the process of recovery to get better.

Next, David didn't deny the incident, the crisis, the loss because it did happen. He just refused to remain in a state of grief. He did not put his car in park, take off the tires, remove the engine, and behave as if life was over. He kept the engine running. His actions said, "I am going to be here for a moment, but then I must move on."

You may be familiar with the statement: "It is a nice place to visit, but I would not want to live there." Well, some time back, I visited Washington, DC, in the summer, and it is a nice place to visit, but it is not my cup of tea, and I do not want to live there.

There is also Broken Arrow, Oklahoma, where I went to Bible school. I graduated on a Friday, and the next morning, I was moving out of the city, and I have not been back since. You may wonder if I liked the city. Visiting was fine, but I had no desire to become a permanent resident. I am sure many would say the same thing about other cities.

The same should hold true when it comes to sorrow. It is a place we will all visit (experience), but we are not supposed to become permanent residents, like squatters.

David's reaction also shows us that he knew how and from whom to get his healing. Notice the progression of what took place. He was sad about his child's illness. Word came to him that the child died. As soon as he heard the news, he picked himself up, bathed and changed his clothes. Then, before he attended to his own home, he went into the house of the Lord to worship. He knew his healing was there. He knew he had to get into the presence of God; it became a priority, a necessity.

I wonder if David felt like taking action in the way he did or if he just knew he should, regardless of how he felt. Hum?

What has been your reaction in a state of mourning? Have you experienced periods when you did not want to pray, read your Bible, or lift your hands and worship God? Have you experienced moments when you did not want to be around Christians or go to church? If your answer is yes, it is understandable. Realize, however, that involving God is what you should do.

Drag your flesh, by faith, out of your house or the place you have been too long, and go into the presence of God. By faith, you pray. By faith, you read the Bible. By faith, you worship God. By faith, you go to church and trust God to change your mourning to joy.

There are many things that we really don't feel like doing, but we must do. I do not always feel like going to work, but I drag my flesh to work. I do not always feel like going to the gym, but I drag my flesh to the gym. Do you ever wake up and think, Oh, I cannot wait to go to the dentist? Of course not! But what do you do? If it is necessary, you drag your flesh out of the house and go to the dentist.

Consider how David recognized that before he could comfort his wife, he first had to be whole and comforted. He had to allow God to minister to him before he could attend to his wife and be a help, not a hindrance, to her.

Anyone who has been on a commercial airplane is likely familiar with the instructions given prior to departure. The instructions are given in case there are issues and oxygen is lost. We are to put our oxygen masks on before assisting someone else.

Not every spouse takes David's approach to heal and recover

after experiencing a loss. As a matter of fact, statistics show that during times of great loss, marriages that once were strong are negatively impacted by the loss. One or both cannot handle the grief, so the pair argue, blame, or turn on each other.

Keep in mind that David's reaction did not mean he didn't love the child he lost or that the child would be forgotten. A loss of any kind is never simply forgotten but is always remembered.

Years ago, my kidney was removed, and there is a scar where the incision was made. If I press on the scar, I do not feel the pain I once felt, but the scar will always remain.

The same can be said about life's scars. We cannot remove the scars left behind by life's experiences, but God can supernaturally take away the sting or the pain associated with those scars.

The Bible states, "Oh death where is thy sting." Death has a sting to it like a bee sting. It hurts; you scream or shout. There is a mark, you rub it, it becomes red, but then, barring any allergies, it's over.

I love the fact that David did not quit on life. He got back in the game. What do I mean by that? He went home, and he ministered to his wife. We do not know how long it took before her period of grief was over. For each of them, it was likely different, like us. At some point, though, the garment of praise replaced the spirit of heaviness (Isaiah 61:3). Once she was restored, the two of them were able to move on together.

In my rendition of David and Bathsheba's story, I imagine the situation went something like this:

> David asked, "Babe, you want to go out for a show tonight?"
>
> Bathsheba replied, "Oh, sure! We haven't been to a show in a long time, not since our loss."
>
> He said, "I'll also take you to your favorite restaurant; how about that?"
>
> "I'd love that," she replied. "We haven't been out since our loss."
>
> "You look beautiful today. You haven't dressed up since our loss," David commented. "I have candy and flowers for you as well."
>
> She smiled and said, "Thank you. It feels good."
>
> When they returned home from their outing, there were rose petals and silk sheets on the bed. David asked, "What do you think; are you ready?"
>
> Bathsheba replied, "Oh my goodness; you've thought of everything," and that night, they conceived Solomon.

You can disagree with my interpretation of the scene, but the point is they did not stop. They pushed past their pain and tried again. They could have decided that the pain of losing a child was too great to try to conceive another. If that had been their decision, they would not have given birth to Solomon, whose name means peace.

Choose to give birth to peace. Extended mourning aborts or delays peace and prolongs grief. What do you need to birth again? What do you need to be delivered?

Consider what the Word of God says in Isaiah 61:3.

> To console those who mourn in Zion, To give them beauty for ashes, The oil of joy for mourning, The garment of praise for the spirit of heaviness; That they may be called trees of righteousness, The planting of the Lord, that He may be glorified.

Although we may experience heartache, the Bible says we will receive the oil of joy for mourning, beauty for the ashes, and when our hearts are heavy, we will receive the garment of praise.

David resumed his role as king. He moved forward in his position and responsibility. It is an assignment God called him to, and David did not allow grief to stop him.

I recently rewatched one of my favorite movies. As I watched, a particular line stood out to me. I thought, *That's going in this book*. The movie is *Gladiator* (2000), and the line from the movie: "Not yet."

There is a scene in the movie where Russell Crowe, who plays the central character, Maximus, in the movie, is having a conversation with another gladiator/slave, Juba. The two are talking about Maximus's son and wife who were killed by the Emperor Commodus. Maximus is experiencing tremendous grief because of his loss. He feels as if he wants to die so that he can be with them. Juba tells Maximus something that stops his tears from flowing and changes his focus. He tells him, "Not yet."

What I believe Juba meant by his statement is that it is not Maximus's time to die. You see, in the movie, Maximus had to conquer the emperor, put Lucius Verus in charge as the new emperor, teach other gladiators how to fight to win, and so much more.

Maybe you need to tell yourself, "Not yet." You are not going to quit; you are not going to die, not yet. You are not going to give up, not yet.

CONSOLING OTHERS

Let me briefly address those who encounter people who are mourning. We should be mindful of what we say when trying to console others. We should not be guilty of holding them back from receiving their healing. If we don't know what to say, we can simply state, "I'm praying for you. How can I help you?"

Refrain from asking what happened when someone is grieving. It may cause them to relive the tragedy once more.

For the most part, people mean well, but some have no bedside manner when it comes to consoling those who are grieving.

I know what I'm talking about because it was true for me when I went through cancer treatments. People would come to me and say, "How do you feel?" I would think, *Don't ask me how I feel because you can't help me.* I would have preferred prayer instead of being asked to relive the battles that I had to face at 9:00 a.m., 11:00 a.m., and 1:00 p.m. I wanted to move forward so that I could receive my healing.

Realize, also, that some who grieve may employ defensive measures to protect their mental state until healing has taken place. It likely has nothing to do with you, so do not take it personally.

CAUSE AND IMPACT

When we experience loss, the cause is not always bearable. For instance, when someone dies as the result of a long-term, terminal illness, loved ones may be more understanding and accepting of death. However, the cause may be less tolerable if a vehicular accident or natural disaster took a life. Such incidents are especially hurtful when the loss could have been avoided. Loss of life caused by reckless driving is one such instance.

Why would someone commit the unconscionable act of street racing, driving while under the influence of alcohol or drugs, or other irresponsible vehicular maneuvers when the potential to injure or kill is at risk?

We know that accidents happen. They occur at work, home, while on vacation, in the park, in a swimming pool; they can happen anywhere. Loss associated with accidents are sometimes the hardest to deal with and most painful of sorrows to endure. Words, poems, hugs, and cries, although appreciated, don't fill the emptiness that is felt.

After the funeral and repast are over and the visits, flowers, and cards have stopped, those impacted are likely left with images of the accident that are stuck on replay in their minds. They may constantly recall the scene of their last encounter with their loved one or visualize repeatedly how he or she appeared in the casket when they were laid to rest. These are often painful realities.

Another thing they may have to deal with is the anger, bitterness, hatred, and unforgiveness they feel toward the person or entity responsible for the loss, as well as the impact their emotional state has on family and friends. There is no enjoyment in the emotional toil. Fury and frustration, however, are prevalent.

Forgiveness toward someone who took the life of a loved one is not something that comes easy, and it may not be on the radar of something to do. However, here is what I know. Considering the words of Jesus, forgiveness is not for someone else; it is for the one who was wronged. When we forgive another person, it benefits us. Bitterness, hatred, and unforgiveness are detrimental to the one harboring the emotions. There is little to no impact on the object of those emotions.

No one gets away with anything. The Bible says, "What a man sows, he reaps." Because of this, it is essential that we allow God to help us release all the negativity we feel toward another. We are to put them into the hands of God rather than try to be the judge or executor of justice. That's not our job.

"To forgive is to set a prisoner free and discover that the prisoner was you."
—Lewis B. Smedes

"It's cheaper to pardon than to resent. Forgiveness saves the expense of anger, the cost of hatred, and the waste of spirit."
—Hannah More

"Patti Davis, the daughter of Ronald Reagan, said that her dad made a lasting impression on her the day after the assassination attempt of 1982. She says, 'The following day my father (Ronald Reagan) said he knew his physical healing was directly dependent on his ability to forgive John Hinckley. By showing me that forgiveness is the key to everything, including physical health and healing, he gave me an example of Christ-like thinking.'"
—The Quote Letter, December, 1996

Forgiveness does not mean we do nothing. A lawyer can be sought, if necessary. We can fight for justice. A support group or campaign that brings awareness to victims and families can still be established.

Not long ago, I attended a MADD meeting (Mothers Against Drunk Drivers). I was there as a San Bernardino Sheriff Chaplin, and performed the invocation for the meeting. As I sat there, I was touched and overwhelmed by the stories from parents and other family members who lost loved ones because someone was intoxicated and irresponsible. The loss they are coping with was completely avoidable.

I sat there trying to understand their pain and the tragedy within their stories. What I noticed was not only the prevailing grief but bitterness, unforgiveness, and hatred toward those who committed the outrageous crime. I could hear and feel their rage. I understood their grief and ill feelings, but I also knew the way for them to begin to heal was along the steady path to forgiveness. My heart went out to them.

I may not know how you feel if this type of loss is your reality. Honestly, many may not. There is, however, one who knows, and He can hold your hand as long as you want. He can walk with you through this season for as long as it takes for you to find some level of normalcy again. Jesus heals the brokenhearted and the begrudged heart.

White Roses symbolize purity, humility, and innocence.

CHAPTER 3

INFLUENCE AND FOCUS

In 2 Samuel 18, we find David experiencing sorrow again as another death occurs in his family—his son Absalom. When David received word from the battlefield that Absalom had died, he was filled with sadness. The Bible reveals the following about David's reaction:

> Then the king was deeply moved, and went up to the chamber over the gate, and wept. And as he went, he said thus: 'O my son Absalom—my son, my son Absalom—if only I had died in your place! O Absalom my son, my son!'
> —2 Samuel 18:33

The story continues in 2 Samuel 19:1-4:

> Joab was told, 'Behold, the king is weeping and mourning for Absalom.' So the victory that day was turned into mourning for all the people. For the people heard it said that day, 'The king is grieved for his son.' And the

people stole back into the city that day, as people who are ashamed steal away when they flee in battle.

But the king covered his face, and the king cried out with a loud voice, 'O my son Absalom! O Absalom, my son, my son!'

The sorrow David felt for Absalom was different from the grief he experienced after losing the child he fathered with Bathsheba. David was so distraught that he lost sight of who he was.

When Joab, the captain of David's army, discovered how David mourned Absalom's death, he went to David. Basically, he told him to get his act together. He told him that his behavior was causing confusion, impeding his leadership, and was not acceptable.

After Absalom's death, David's reaction sent a strong message to his people. It was as if his life was no longer worth living. His perpetual grief was becoming destructive. Do you understand why? It's because David lost focus. His focus was no longer on his position as king. He was not ruling and reigning during his grieving period. He was neglecting his responsibilities. It was as if he didn't care about his other children, his kingdom, his future, or the call on his life.

Thank God for Joab. We all need people like Joab in our lives to come and speak the truth to us when we wander too far or take things too far. There comes a time when people need to hold our hands and speak encouraging words, and then there comes a time when people need to lift us up out of the place of mourning and say, "Enough is enough!" Joabs shake us back into purpose.

Joabs let us know when our actions are becoming destructive. They remind us that our lives are not ours and that there is a life worth living. They remind us that others are depending on us. They remind us that there are dreams in our hearts and visions for our lives. If they recognize the signs, they aren't afraid to tell us that we're headed toward an emotional breakdown and that we'll be stuck in that state for far too long if we don't take action to avoid it.

Joabs in the lives of Davids are to pray for them, stay in proximity to them, watch after and check in on them. That may look like taking them out to lunch to talk or helping them with funeral arrangements or other personal affairs such as making a decision regarding their loved one's belongings. That may look like allowing them time to vent and release their emotions with a non-judgmental attitude. They are to love them. This is a key antidote for recovery.

Davids should not isolate themselves but should find community—a Joab to talk to, vent to, and think things through.

I make the following statement compassionately and in the best way possible. We cannot afford to allow a person or a possession, whatever and whoever it may be, to have a greater influence in our lives than Jesus Christ. Our love for Christ has to be greater than our love for anyone or anything.

When someone says, "I can't live without you," "I can't live without them," "I can't live without these things," "I don't want to live any longer," or "My life is over without him," whether they realize it or not, they may be on the verge of worshiping that individual or thing. I know it sounds hard or harsh, but I think you realize there is truth there.

Jesus said in Matthew 10:37 (NLT), "If you love your father or mother more than you love Me, you are not worthy of being mine; or if you love your son or daughter more than Me, you are not worthy of being mine."

Not too long ago, I was blindsided by a tragic announcement. I had just finished preaching the first of two Sunday morning services, and was sitting in my office awaiting the start of the second service. I noticed a text message alert on my phone and looked down to read it. The message was from a friend, and he was informing me that my pastor and spiritual father, someone that I had known for nearly thirty years, had died. The first words out of my mouth were, "Oh my God!"

I owe a lot of my ministry successes to my spiritual father. He was a difference-maker in my life in many ways and certainly instrumental in the body of Christ. Losing him was a tremendous loss for me and others.

Immediately, I called the friend who sent the message to get details about what happened. As I listened to him explain what he knew, I began to feel cold and alone, and tears began to flow from my eyes. I was shocked, confused, and overwhelmed by the news. Time seemed to slow down during that rush of grief I was experiencing.

After the call, I began to recall the conversations I had and the memories I shared with my pastor, mentor, hero, and friend. I thought to myself, *I just spoke to him*. We had planned to get together in the weeks to come.

The start of the second service came faster than anticipated; I had to take my place in the sanctuary to preach once more. I composed myself, reentered the sanctuary, and preached my sermon for a second time. Although still sad about what had taken place, shifting my focus toward my responsibility in that moment was the right thing for me to do.

I felt off or odd in the days that followed. I cried a few times over the loss of my dear friend. I occasionally think about his influence on my life, especially when something triggers a memory, and I even dream about him. I can genuinely say I'm extremely grateful to God for allowing my spiritual father and me to share life. The impact he made will never be forgotten.

Know that loving someone is good and healthy. God designed us to love. I believe the verse in Matthew is saying that the love we have for someone or something should not be greater than our love for Christ. God understands how difficult it is when we lose a loved one or something of value. Still, we are not to make them idols of worship where we esteem them greater than the creator of our existence, and they should not have more influence in our lives than Jesus does.

There is another story involving David and sorrow. 1 Samuel tells of an incident that caused David's heart to grieve. His home was destroyed, and his family was taken captive by his enemy.

Let's take a look at 1 Samuel 30:1-2:

> Now it happened when David and his men came to Ziklag on the third day that the Amalekites had invaded the South and Ziklag, and attacked Ziklag and burned it with fire, and had taken captive the women and those who were there, from small to great; they did not kill anyone but carried them away and went their way.

Ziklag is where David lived with upwards of 600 men (his army), their wives, and possessions. The Amalekites attacked Ziklag when David and his men were away. The story continues in verses 3-8:

> So David and his men came to the city, and there it was, burned with fire; and their wives, their sons, and their daughters had been taken captive. Then David and the people who were with him lifted up their voices and wept, until they had no more power to weep....
>
> Now David was greatly distressed, for the people spoke of stoning him, because the soul of all the people was grieved, every man for his sons and his daughters. But David strengthened himself in the Lord his God....
>
> So David inquired of the Lord, saying, 'Shall I pursue this troop? Shall I overtake them?' And He answered him, 'Pursue, for you shall surely overtake them and without fail recover all.'

In this situation, David briefly wore the garment of grief and then took it off. While everyone was grieving, everyone was losing it; everyone was talking and acting irrationally or hysterically, and everything was chaotic—while there was confusion and drama—notice what David did. The passage tells us, "David strengthened himself in the Lord his God." He put on his new garments: the garment of strength and the garment of courage. They were the garments that would put him in a position to recover what the enemy stole or intended. He would recover what the devastation was keeping from him.

Here is what we can learn from this story of David: We cannot hang around people who are stuck on being sad and expect to be healed. Sometimes we must choose, in love, to turn away from those who will hinder us. We may have to decide not to return the phone call or text message or accept the lunch invitations because our priority is to be healed. Some people may not want us to heal, or their influence won't allow us to heal. David had to make that choice. He diverted his focus from those who wept to the God who would help him recover all.

It's interesting to read that sometimes Jesus had to take an individual out of their familiar environment for healing to take place. While in Bethsaida, He led a blind man out of the village and healed him (Mark 8:22-26 NIV). Could there have been something or someone in the village hindering him from receiving his healing?

Sometimes, God does the same thing with you and me. When we experience a change in our surroundings (associations, environments), God can begin to heal our lives.

The man in Bethsaida, for a moment, left his normal environment, went somewhere new, and was healed. What does that say to you?

I have a friend who lost his wife. We've been friends for years. During a conversation with him, about seven months after his wife's death, he revealed something to me.

My friend said, "Diego, guess what I did today?"

I asked, "What did you do?"

"I bought brand-new furniture," he replied. "I had to get rid of the old furniture because it represented so many memories. I also cleared out all of my wife's clothes, and I have very limited pictures of her in the house because I have to move on."

If you're struggling through a similar situation, know that I'm not telling you to do the same thing my friend did. What I am telling you is to consider what you're doing or not doing to receive your healing or what may be stopping it or slowing it down. Inventory and evaluate your life. Assess our habits, moods, emotions, and words.

Sometimes, you must move items out of the house, store the pictures, and clean out the closet. Sometimes, you can't visit the gravesite to honor the memory of your loved one because it keeps you back from being restored. Everyone is different, so you must be honest with yourself about what you can handle and what you can't handle. Recognize how, where, and what you do affects you emotionally.

Furthermore, you must learn how to dream again, and you must learn how to live on by creating new memories, new victories, and new experiences. I'm not saying you have to forget the past, but I am asking you to remember God in the midst of your situation.

Lastly, in the story, I noticed that David and his friends got their families back and recovered the property the enemy stole. They did not, however, get their homes back. They were burned to the ground.

Fire devastated David's home, similar to the wildfires that devastated parts of Maui in 2023 and parts of the Los Angeles area in 2025. An overwhelming number of homes and businesses were destroyed during both instances.

So, what did David, his men, and their families do? Did they rebuild? Did they move to new homes or different cities? Regardless of whether they decided to rebuild or move on, David, his men, and their families recovered all, just as the Lord said.

White Daffodils symbolize rebirth and new beginnings.

CHAPTER 4

CYCLES AND SETBACKS

There is a condition called "broken heart syndrome." The Cleveland Clinic (Broken Heart Syndrome: Clevelandclinic.org) provides the following description:

> Broken heart syndrome is a short-term condition where some of your heart muscle weakens rapidly. This typically happens after a sudden physical or emotional stressor.
>
> [A] weak heart muscle can disrupt your heart's supply of blood and its ability to pump. If your heart isn't pumping well, that harms your whole body. Every cell in your body relies on the steady supply of oxygen that your blood carries.

An example provided in the article as a "sudden emotional stressor" is "grief from the death of a loved one." It can also occur as a result of another emotionally devastating or "meaningful loss."

An article by Johns Hopkins Medicine (Broken Heart Syndrome | Johns Hopkins Medicine) states the following:

> The symptoms of broken heart syndrome can mimic symptoms of a heart attack, including chest pain, shortness of breath, sweating, and dizziness. These symptoms may begin as soon as minutes or as long as hours after an emotionally or physically stressful event.

Broken heart syndrome can be experienced when one mate dies and, shortly thereafter, the other mate dies. The second mate to pass may have been in perfect health, but the stress of losing a spouse produced heart fatigue, which resulted in heart failure and death. It may have happened to a couple you know, or you may have heard about a couple in the public arena.

Doug Flutie, a former NFL quarterback, lost his dad, and one day later, his mom died. There was a famous actress named Mary Tamm who was married to Marcus Ringnose. Marcus gave the eulogy during the service for Mary Tamm, and the next day, he died. There is also a story involving June and Johnny Cash, who died four months apart.

Please understand that I don't have an issue with individuals impacted by broken heart syndrome if the parties are advanced in years, have lived a full life, and God has nothing else for them to do. However, there are those who are full of life and have years ahead of them who lose hope and feel they have no purpose amid loss. Sadly, they don't recognize that God has something more for them.

Wikipedia has an interesting article on a condition known as Complicated Grief Disorder. It states the following:

> In psychiatry, complicated grief disorder (CGD) is a proposed disorder for those who are significantly and functionally impaired by prolonged grief symptoms for at least one month after six months of bereavement. Complicated grief is considered when an individual's ability to resume normal activities and responsibilities is continually disrupted beyond six months of bereavement. Six months is considered to be the appropriate point of CGD consideration, since studies show that most people are able to integrate bereavement into their lives by this time.

There can be an imbalance that involves excessive crying and overwhelming sorrow. For those struggling with it, there seems to be no end to grief. The individual is completely stopped by it and accepts no path to recovery. It's when the sting of the loss overpowers the individual, and the event becomes debilitating and destructive.

I say the following with genuine compassion. There comes a point when we must say, "I cannot continue to feel this way and form negative thoughts or actions. I am not crying about this anymore. I have been crying over this too long." To do that, we must put our pain and sorrow in proper perspective to deal with it and seek ways to recover. We must give our pain to someone who can help us, and that person is Jesus. As I mentioned, we must understand there is a time for mourning, but there is also an expiration date.

You may ask, "Is it possible to mourn people, things, and situations longer than we should?" The answer is yes. When we prolong grief, it can become unhealthy and hinder us from moving forward and healing. When that occurs, we don't fulfill the destiny, calling, assignment, dreams, visions, goals, and purposes God has given us.

For those struggling to overcome grief, realize that God is not done with you, and that is something you must accept as truth despite how you feel or what you want.

Psalm 77 was written by a man named Asaph. The chapter speaks of the distress birthed during a time of great anguish for him and his family, possibly during the Babylonian conquest of Judah. Great calamity had fallen upon the nation due to unfaithfulness and maybe indifference toward God. Asaph was likely experiencing sleep-deprived nights, feelings of hopelessness, and helplessness. There was truly nothing pretty to look forward to. Nothing was exciting to anticipate and nothing to laugh about.

I ask you to consider why the psalm has been preserved for centuries. If I can be forthright, I believe it was preserved for us. It is a passage we can reflect on in moments of loss and grief, when everything feels challenging, where maybe faith is low, fear is rising, and trusting God seems impossible. Like Asaph, we may feel like God is distant or that His promises do not work and are not for us, fueling sleepless nights.

Know that God loves us and wants us to pour out our honest anguish and be transparent with Him, no matter how raw, real, and unfiltered it may be. Like Asaph, we should look to our past to remember and retrace God's faithfulness, love, and grace. He has provided for us in the past and can bring hope to our present situation. We must trust Him to do so.

At times, we may feel like hope and change are out of reach. We may feel like we're not being comforted and not getting better, like Asaph, and we may start to believe that nothing will change. We may even get to a place where our soul refuses (denies, rejects, disdains) comfort (recovery). Hum? This is a light bulb moment. I would like to briefly tackle this thought.

A person who has experienced a loss can get to a place where he or she refuses to be comforted. Isaiah 61:3 talks about a garment of praise as a spiritual weapon used to battle against the anguish of grief during times of despair. Isaiah identifies the anguish as a "spirit of heaviness." This is far greater than just an emotion or sensation. It is what Isaiah has labeled it as: a "spirit."

2 Timothy 1:7 talks about a "spirit of fear," Mark 9:25 talks about a "deaf and dumb spirit," Numbers 5:12 talks about a "spirit of jealousy," 1 Chronicles 18:22 talks about a "lying spirit." The "spirit of heaviness," like the others, is a demonic attack against someone's life. Its objective is to forbid or oppose an individual from recovering. Simple discouragement, despair, loneliness, and grief are the starting points, but they can grow stronger.

The longer a demonic attack is tolerated, justified, excused, and accepted as a forever situation, the longer it is empowered. It's like a thought that evolves into an action. It's like a belief that develops into a lifestyle. It's like a shopping spree that turns into hoarding. It's like an isolated incident that becomes an obsession.

Have you ever met someone who did not want to change? Have you ever met someone who does not want help? Have you ever met someone who does not want to be a better version of themself? The individual seems to find comfort in their misery.

I know people who can walk, but because they are a bit overweight, they choose to move around on a scooter. They believe they need the scooter; they've grown accustomed to it. Could this describe someone who refuses to be comforted?

When someone refuses to be comforted, not realizing it, they are accommodating the spirit of heaviness and making it feel welcome. They are allowing it to move in with its relatives and squat for a while. The person does not have the desire to evict or eradicate it.

Refusing to be comforted may be saying, "I don't want to get better." "I don't deserve to get better." "I like the emotional place I am in."

In the book of Joshua, we read about God's charge to Joshua after Moses' death.

> After the death of Moses the servant of the Lord, the Lord said to Joshua son of Nun, Moses' aide: 'Moses my servant is dead. Now then, you and all these people, get ready to cross the Jordan River into the land I am about to give to them—to the Israelites.'
> —Joshua 1:1-2 (NIV)

The story of Moses and Joshua is a great example from which

we can learn. These men spent forty years together and were lifelong friends. I am sure Joshua grieved when Moses died, but when God spoke to him, after giving him time to grieve, He challenged him to move forward and lead the people as Moses led them. If Joshua had given up and not done as God directed, he would not have inherited the Promised Land. He and the children of Israel would not have fulfilled the destiny that God set for them.

Understand that by not continuing the grieving process longer than you should, you are not saying you have forgotten your loved one or that you don't miss them. You are simply indicating that you will redirect your emotions to what is ahead, on promises in your future.

Excuse me for a moment for being presumptuous. I believe the enemy has an agenda in your grief, and that is to take you out of the will of God. He wants to keep you where you are or lead you down a dark and destructive path lined with depression, isolation, bitterness, self-pity, and self-harm.

Just think for a moment. What would the enemy like you to do right now? Who would he want you to become? What would he not want you to do? The Bible challenges us to not give place or give in to the enemy's agenda (Ephesians 4:27).

In the face of grief, ask this question: "Are there any inflated negative emotions, or can I deflate any destructive emotions?"

In Jude 1:20, we read, "But you, beloved, building yourselves up on your most holy faith, praying in the Holy Spirit...."

Pray in the Spirit because sometimes your flesh does not want to pray, or you don't know what to say. Sometimes, you don't have the emotional strength to pray in your understanding, so pray in the Spirit with the help of the Holy Spirit.

I am an advocate of praying in the Spirit. I also recognize not everyone believes in praying in the Spirit. My life, however, has been established on this belief over the 40+ years of my Christian faith. I went through some of the most hellish days in my life during my bout with cancer. I can't imagine enduring what I experienced without the ability to pray in the Spirit. I don't know how I would have made it through some of those tough days. I will admit, there were days I had to dig down deep inside to find the strength to pray.

One of my favorite verses on prayer is found in Romans 8:26. It states the following:

> Likewise the Spirit helps us in our weakness. For we do not know what we should pray for as we ought, but the Spirit Himself makes intercession for us with groanings which cannot be uttered.

When we don't know how or what to pray for what is in our hearts, we pray in the Spirit, in faith. The Spirit appeals to God on our behalf.

You should also encourage yourself by confessing the Word of God over your life. Reciting the following scriptures was a part of my routine:

"I shall not die, but live, and declare the works of the Lord."

—Psalm 118:17

"And we know that all things work together for good to those who love God, to those who are the called according to His purpose."

—Romans 8:28

"I will restore health to you and heal you of your wounds...."

—Jeremiah 30:17

It is important to confess the Word of God over your life. I recommend that you commit as many scriptures as you can to memory. Hebrews 10:23 states, "Let us hold fast the confession of our hope without wavering, for He who promised is faithful."

I want to share an astonishing story about a man named Horatio Spafford who lived in the 1800s. He was a devout Christian who understood the importance of taking off the garment of mourning.

Horatio resided in Chicago. He was a very successful lawyer, a real estate investor, and a good man. He was married and had five children—one son and four daughters.

In the late 1860s, Horatio's son died. In 1871, the year of the great Chicago fire, he lost his business and all his real estate investments as a result of the fire.

While trying to recover from the losses he endured, he decided to send his family on vacation. He was delayed due to business transactions, so he put his wife and four daughters on a ship, kissed them goodbye, and sent them to Europe. He planned to join them not long after their departure.

In the middle of the Atlantic, the ship collided with another vessel. All four daughters drowned in the ocean. Horatio received a telegram from his wife that stated, "I alone am saved."

Not long after Horatio received notice of what took place, he boarded a ship to go and comfort his wife. During his journey, the captain brought him forward and said, "We believe this is the area where your daughters drowned when the vessels collided." At that moment, Horatio took a piece of paper and began to pen the words of a song.

Years passed, and he and his wife had three more children—two girls and a boy. Sadly, that son died as well.

Horatio Spafford experienced much tragedy during his life. But the words of the song he wrote in 1873, as he stood on the ship overlooking the place where his four daughters drowned, reveal to us how he dealt with sorrow. The following are the lyrics to Horatio's song, "It Is Well with My Soul:"

> *When peace like a river, attendeth my way,*
> *When sorrows like sea billows roll;*
> *Whatever my lot, thou hast taught me to know,*
> *It is well; it is well, with my soul.*

Refrain:
It is well with my soul,
It is well; it is well with my soul.

Though Satan should buffet, though trials should come,
Let this blest assurance control,
That Christ has regarded my helpless estate,
And hath shed His own blood for my soul.

My sin, oh, the bliss of this glorious thought!
My sin, not in part but the whole,
Is nailed to the cross, and I bear it no more,
Praise the Lord, praise the Lord, O my soul.

For me, be it Christ, be it Christ hence to live:
If Jordan above me shall roll,
No pang shall be mine, for in death as in life
Thou wilt whisper Thy peace to my soul!

But, Lord, 'tis for Thee, for Thy coming we wait,
The sky, not the grave, is our goal;
Oh, trump of the angel! Oh, voice of the Lord!
Blessed hope, blessed rest of my soul!

And Lord, haste the day when my faith shall be sight,
The clouds be rolled back as a scroll;
The trump shall resound, and the Lord shall descend,
A song in the night, oh my soul!

Maybe you are struggling to recover because you have been grieving for years. You feel that after an extended period, you are not getting better but worse. Maybe you are feeling that something other than you is controlling your emotions or decisions. Maybe everyone close to you who loves you has pointed out that something is abnormal about how long your grief has lasted. Perhaps it has changed your personality—how you used to be. If this is you, please declare the prayer at the end of this book over your life.

Whatever you are facing today, or when you come face to face with sadness and grief, sing this song or recite the lyrics, or write and sing your own song that God may give you, especially when you feel that sorrow is getting the best of you. No one has to hear it or hear you sing it, and it may not win a Grammy award.

Horatio Spafford wrote the words to his song from his heart as he viewed the place where his daughters died. Like Horatio, it will be well with your soul when you turn to Jesus, who is more than enough for any situation, sorrow, or immeasurable grief.

Casa Blanca Lilies symbolize positivity and celebration.

CHAPTER 5

JESUS' ACQUAINTANCE WITH GRIEF

The Bible reveals that Jesus knew how it felt to be human. He was sympathetic and understood human weaknesses and temptations. We read the following in Hebrews 4:15-16 (AMP):

> For we do not have a High Priest who is unable to sympathize and understand our weaknesses and temptations, but One who has been tempted [knowing exactly how it feels to be human] in every respect as we are, yet without [committing any] sin.
>
> Therefore, let us [with privilege] approach the throne of grace [that is, the throne of God's gracious favor] with confidence and without fear, so that we may receive mercy [for our failures] and find [His amazing] grace to help in time of need [an appropriate blessing, coming just at the right moment].

The Lord understands grief and sorrow more than you can imagine because He experienced it. Jesus experienced grief when

His relative John the Baptist was executed. They were only six months apart in age and no doubt the families were close and experienced life together. Likely, there were visits, conversations, laughter, memories, and good times they shared.

The Bible records in Matthew 14:3-10 that John was imprisoned and beheaded by Herod the tetrarch because John rebuked him of his marriage to Herodias, his brother's wife. What a terrible and horrific way to die.

After burying his body, John's disciples went to Jesus to tell Him what occurred (verse 12). The Bible tells us that when Jesus heard the news, He left in a boat to a remote area to be alone (verse 13). Jesus wanted some alone time, quiet time, all-by-himself time, check-out time.

There is another account of how Jesus expressed Himself amid loss. The shortest verse in the Bible is John 11:35, which states, "Jesus wept." This reaction was in response to Lazarus' death before he was raised back to life. Although brief, as it relates to the subject of grief, it speaks loudly and profoundly. It says it all!

When I think about Jesus weeping and feeling sorrow, I recognize that His reaction and emotions speak to us and give us permission to feel the way we feel. His reaction also says that what we are feeling is real, not made up. He absolutely validates our tears. Otherwise, Jesus, who is perfection on display, would not have reacted in that way.

When we grieve, we experience real feelings, real thoughts, real concerns, and they provoke those precious tears. Those we lost were loved, special, and precious, which is why we cry uncontrollably and profusely sometimes.

Amid grief, Jesus still displayed compassion toward others. He didn't allow what He felt to deter Him from the purpose for which He was sent. In Matthew 14:13-14 (NLT), we read the following:

> But the crowds heard where He was headed and followed on foot from many towns. Jesus saw the huge crowd as He stepped from the boat, and He had compassion on them and healed their sick.

I love the Bible. It says so much that cannot be ignored. It speaks directly to our needs.

Now, take a look at how a different passage describes the Lord. We read the following in Isaiah 53:3-5:

> He is despised and rejected by men, A man of sorrows and acquainted with grief. And we hid, as it were, our faces from Him. He was despised, and we did not esteem Him.

> Surely, He has borne our griefs And carried our sorrows; Yet we esteemed Him stricken, smitten by God, and afflicted.

> But He was wounded for our transgressions; He was bruised for our iniquities; The chastisement for our peace was upon Him, and by His stripes we are healed.

Notice the phrases "acquainted with grief" and "borne our griefs." Jesus identified with and went through what you are going through. He felt what you are feeling.

What is so amazing about the verse in Isaiah is that it reveals that we no longer have to carry the weight of our sorrows because Jesus already did that for us on the cross. The Bible tells us, "By His stripes we are healed." He did all of that for you and me so that we can know and believe there is no situation where Jesus is not enough. He carried your sorrow. Maybe you need to repeat that over and over until it sinks in deep.

If you don't know how to move from a place of despair, I encourage you to depend on Jesus because He is more than enough. I also challenge you to ask Jesus to heal and restore you by confessing Jeremiah 17:14 (NLT), "O LORD, if you heal me, I will be truly healed; if you save me, I will be truly saved. My praises are for you alone!" And according to Jeremiah 30:17 (NLT), this is the Lord's response to you, "I will give you back your health and heal your wounds."

Ask yourself: If He bore it, should you act like He did not? If He bore it, how should you think or react to what you are feeling? The answer is that it should bring overwhelming liberty and understanding to your heart.

Here is another question: When is Jesus not enough for you to be restored?" The answer is NEVER! He is always enough.

Do you know why Jesus is enough amid your sorrow and pain? It's because He promises you healing and power, He promises you His presence, and He promises to help you. When the enemy comes and lies to you, saying that Jesus isn't enough, you need to tell him that Jesus is more than enough.

At the end of the day, no one other than Jesus can completely identify with your grief or precisely say the right words. No one else knows exactly how you feel except Him. He is the one who can help you heal completely. He has experienced your grief, and He is the one who knows the depth, height, length, and breadth of it. He knows you. He knows how to renew, repair, and rebuild you.

Keep in mind that your loved one was dear to Jesus as well, and He will stay with you until the very end of your recovery, no matter how long it takes. He doesn't charge by the hour.

Daisies symbolize purity and new beginnings.

CHAPTER 6

A NEW NORMAL

People have survived some of life's most tragic circumstances, such as being stranded in the ocean, being trapped in a desert, a large percentage of their body being burned, or using a knife to cut off a limb lodged between rocks. The secret is the will to live and do whatever it takes to live, not necessarily one day at a time, but one second, minute, or hour at a time. It is choosing to create or accept a new normal amid tragedy.

You can still run, walk, and race, even when impaired. In Genesis 32:25, 32, we read the following:

> Now when He saw that He did not prevail against him, He touched the socket of his hip; and the socket of Jacob's hip was out of joint as He wrestled with him.

> Therefore, to this day the children of Israel do not eat the muscle that shrank, which is on the hip socket, because He touched the socket of Jacob's hip in the muscle that shrank.

We read that Jacob's encounter left him with a limp, and he had it for the remainder of his life. He was around age 97 when it occurred, and Jacob lived to be 147 years old. He lived approximately 50 years with a limp and did so much more living.

Have you ever watched the Special Olympics or Paralympics? It involves events where men and women compete in various events, and some do so with a limp, which may be due to a prosthetic limb. Their limp doesn't stop them from getting to the starting line and racing. Some of these athletes run marathons (26.2 miles).

Jacky Hunt-Broersma is in the Guinness World Book of Records for running 104 marathons in 104 consecutive days as an amputee. She wears a prosthetic leg (below the knee) and runs with a limp.

What am I trying to tell you? Life is not over, even though you may feel like a limb is missing or you're walking with a limp. You still have a God-given purpose and a race to run and live to the glory of God. Muster up the courage with God's grace and help. He will get you to the daily starting line, so run!

There is an old hymn composed by an anonymous writer in 1880. The following are the lyrics.

> *We are soldiers in the army.*
> *We have to fight although we have to cry.*
> *We've got to hold up the bloodstained banner.*
> *We've got to hold it up until we die.*

Let me draw your attention to a particular phrase in the hymn: "...fight (engage in battle, war, combat) although we have to cry (shed tears, feel sad, be sorrowful)." That may be where you are. Maybe crying is your mode of comfort. Perhaps the lyrics provide an answer to what you need to do.

It is okay to cry but not okay to stop the fight. You are a soldier, and through the fight, you will overcome.

Tears are temporary, and they declare that you are alive. Tears say that you are human and your body is responding to something. Tears may say you have good memories and experiences associated with the feelings that draw out those tears. Tears say you were loved or were in love with someone. Tears may say that your heart is in the right place. Tears may say, "I miss my loved one, but I am happy that they no longer have to suffer." Their reward is in Heaven, and it is to be with Jesus, and you are happy about that.

I lost a close friend of mine during the COVID-19 crisis. We were the best friends, someone I had known for over thirty-five years. We went on vacations together, we worked out together, and we went on walks. We logged thousands of hours of deep, emotional conversations and shared our greatest sorrows, pain, and losses in life. There was nothing we didn't share with one another.

From my perspective, my friend was in fairly good health and definitely full of life. However, during the COVID crisis in 2020, he was rushed to the hospital after experiencing a critical health event. He was in the hospital for over a month and was placed on a ventilator in a comatose state.

Because of the pandemic, being by his side in the hospital was virtually impossible. Because I knew the hospital administrator, I was granted two opportunities to visit my friend briefly.

After several weeks of praying and believing for his recovery, I lost my friend; he never regained consciousness.

He had dreams and hopes to fulfill. We often talked about his retirement. I remember thinking that his precious family and beloved friends couldn't grieve properly because of the "social distancing" protocols put in place during the pandemic. Those were odd times for many.

I cannot completely recall the details of everything that occurred during the ordeal. I feel like I'm in a fog when I try to recollect the events. I have asked myself, "Did I block it out?" "Did everything happen as fast as it seems?"

If you are wondering, the answer is yes; I still think about my friend as well as my pastor and spiritual father, and I do experience sadness, which springs up occasionally. I have unanswered questions about each one's death. One thing, though, that I know for sure is that I will see them again in Heaven, and that brings comfort and joy to my heart.

As we grieve, there comes a point when we must accept that a new normal is what's next in our healing process. A new normal can be a new temperament, new perspective, new routine or habit. It is a transition from what was to what can or will be.

What will your new normal look like? What will you do next? Where will you go? Who will you do life with, even though you don't have your partner, friend, relative, or mate with whom you used to do life?

New norms may include downsizing or upscaling, vacationing, traveling, retiring, or returning to work. New norms may consist of adjusting to doing things alone, such as driving, eating, sleeping, or watching television alone. No matter what your new normal is, choose to be a survivor, an overcomer. You are a thriver; you are a conqueror.

At the appropriate time, allow God to lift the mourning garment and replace it with the garments of faith, hope, and love. Welcome the time to heal, the time to laugh, the time to dance, and the time to plant new dreams and experience a bright future.

To help you through your sorrow, consider writing a letter to someone, something, or yourself to bring closure. Expressing your feelings in writing may prove to be beneficial and liberating.

Hydrangea symbolizes devotion, understanding, and true friendship.

CHAPTER 7

THE GREATER GAIN

The scriptures encourage us as believers that one day, we will be reunited with our loved ones. Our hope is that death is not the end but a brand-new beginning in Heaven. Death is the beginning of an eternal life. It is an existence free from sickness, sorrow, heartache, evil, stress, failure, and disappointment. It really is a grand graduation, promotion, and a "to be continued."

1 Thessalonians 4:13-14 (ESV) states the following:

> But we do not want you to be uninformed, brothers, about those who are asleep, that you may not grieve as others do who have no hope. For since we believe that Jesus died and rose again, even so, through Jesus, God will bring with him those who have fallen asleep.

I love how God calls death falling asleep. When you were a young child, did you ever fall asleep in the car? Maybe after a visit to your grandparent's home, you fell asleep, and your mom or dad had to pick you up into their arms and carry you to your bed. When you awoke the next morning, you could not recall who carried you or how you got there.

God's word reveals that when we die, it is as simple as falling asleep. You close your eyes and then open them to awake in a different location. Dying or falling asleep on this side of heaven is allowing God to pick you up and take you into His presence. Using this simple metaphor, consider the following thoughts:

1. How many of us love our sleep, power naps, cat naps, snooze time, siesta time, and night slumbers? We love it, don't we?

2. We do not fear sleeping. We are not afraid to sleep. We are not frightened because it is a place of comfort.

3. We do not worry about whether we will wake up. There is no anxiety or concern. We are at peace, right?

4. Would you say sleeping is a good thing or a bad thing? Most of the time, it is good. It is like a well-deserved reward.

5. Sleep is transitional. It is an exchange of tiredness for energy. It is the ending of one day and the beginning of another. It is a finish that leads to a new start.

6. Sleeping is a place of total stillness, quietness, serenity, and rest. There are no pressures or stresses. Isn't that true?

7. Asleep is when your best dreams occur—fun, laughter,

joy, and conquering. Sounds good, right?

8. Sleep is a state in which the body begins to heal, repair, and create new cells. It is the picture of renewal. How much more will the transition to Heaven bring us?

I believe the Bible got it right. I always look forward to sleeping. I have even planned out my sleep. I have plans...one day, I will go to sleep and wake up in Jesus' presence. Yippy! We are dying to sleep.

It has been said that the late great Prime Minister of Great Britain, Winston Churchill, expressed before he died that he wanted "Taps" played at his funeral, which signified that his earthly life was over. In addition, the trumpet was to play "Reveille," which signified his new life in Heaven had begun.

Another illustration that drives the point I'm making is that in times of old when utensils were not readily available after a good meal (no additional or disposable utensils), one would keep their fork, which was the only utensil. The host, once the guests finished the main course, would tell them, "Hold onto your fork." That meant dessert, or something better than what they already consumed, was on its way.

It has been established through scripture that we do not grieve as those who do not know Christ, those who have no hope. The Bible is clear and truthful, without error, when it states, "To be absent from the body is to be present with the Lord." We, as believers, arrive in Heaven to be reunited with loved ones who have preceded us. Best of all, we get to see and experience

Jesus in all of His glory, majesty, love, and splendor forever and forever. Wow! There is more to come.

Philippians 1:21 states, "To die is gain." What is it that we gain or acquire? What are the advantages, benefits, or profits? What has Jesus been preparing (John 14:2-3) for His family (children, believers, followers)? We gain Heaven, which is God's home that He shares with us. Just like Dorothy from the movie, "The Wizard of Oz," or E.T. from the movie "E.T. The Extra-Terrestrial," we get to go home. Our home in Heaven is the better that awaits us.

Psalm 116:15 (KJV) states, "Precious in the sight of the Lord is the death of His saints." Notice that the word "precious" is used in describing the death of a Christian. That's probably not a word that one would use at a funeral to describe death, but God does. He says it is precious (very dear, special, of great value) to Him.

The following are a few scriptures that describe what we gain when we arrive at our home in Heaven. May these passages bring healing to your hurt as well as assurance and confidence to your faith.

Revelation 14:13 - The gain of eternal rest

> "Then I heard a voice from heaven saying to me, 'Write: Blessed are the dead who die in the Lord from now on.' 'Yes,' says the Spirit, 'that they may rest from their labors, and their works follow them.'"

- Free from all doubt, anxiety, fear, negativity, heaviness, tiredness, performance, competition, stress, and pressure.

Revelations 22:1-5 - The gain of radiance

"And he showed me a pure river of water of life, clear as crystal, proceeding from the throne of God and of the Lamb. In the middle of its street, and on either side of the river, was the tree of life, which bore twelve fruits, each tree yielding its fruit every month. The leaves of the tree were for the healing of the nations. And there shall be no more curse, but the throne of God and of the Lamb shall be in it, and His servants shall serve Him. They shall see His face, and His name shall be on their foreheads. There shall be no night there: They need no lamp nor light of the sun, for the Lord God gives them light. And they shall reign forever and ever."

- Tremendous, spectacular, and overwhelming beauty.
- No more ugliness, filth, disappointment, brokenness, or poverty.
- Glorious, amazing, indescribable, "I'm going to cry" moments, and "I don't deserve this" moments.

Revelations 21:4 - The gain of limitlessness

"And God will wipe away every tear from their eyes; there shall be no more death, nor sorrow, nor crying. There shall be no more pain, for the former things have passed away."

- Amazing and unlimited strength and abilities. No disability or deformity.
- Freedom from sorrow, tears, pain, sickness, disease, loss, and remorse.

Revelations 5:9 - The gain of rejoicing

"And they sang a new song, saying:
'You are worthy to take the scroll,
And to open its seals;
For You were slain,
And have redeemed us to God by Your blood
Out of every tribe and tongue and people and nation.'"

- Joy, dancing, excitement, enthusiasm, praise, exhilaration.
- Constant smile on your face.
- No more devil to deal with.

Revelations 20:11 - The gain of relationship

"Then I saw a great white throne and Him who sat on it, from whose face the earth and the heaven fled away. And there was found no place for them."

- No more separation, distance, distractions, or barriers between you and Jesus.
- A face-to-face relationship allows us to touch, see, and hear Him; it is intimacy.
- No more part-time visitations, but permanently in His presence.

John 14:2 - The gain of residency

"In My Father's house are many mansions; if it were not so, I would have told you. I go to prepare a place for you."

- A permanent, eternal home—a dwelling that is debt-free, can't face bankruptcy, and requires no mortgage or refinancing.
- It is better than ocean-view property.

Revelations 2:7 - The gain of rewards

"He who has an ear, let him hear what the Spirit says to the churches. To him who overcomes I will give to eat from the tree of life, which is in the midst of the Paradise of God."

- Acknowledgments, crowns, pleasure, riches, promotions, recompense, awards, and honor.
- It is better than a paycheck.

1 Thessalonians 4:17 - The gain of reunion

"Then we who are alive and remain shall be caught up together with them in the clouds to meet the Lord in the air. And thus we shall always be with the Lord."

- Being together with no time limitations. Seeing each other, hanging out, the biggest celebration you will ever attend.
- It is better than a family reunion.

John 11:25 - The gain is real

> "Jesus said to her, 'I am the resurrection and the life. He who believes in Me, though he may die, he shall live.'"

- It is not made-up, fictitious, bogus, fabricated, or a sham.
- It is true, certain, absolute, and guaranteed.
- "Pinch me; is this real?" Yes, it is!

With this limited insight into Heaven, where your loved one goes and we will be, do you see it as an advantage or disadvantage? Is this a gain or loss? Is this precious or of no value to you?

Recognize that for believers, your loved one is not a part of your past. They are a part of an unending future. There is truly a lot more time, conversations, and affection to come with them.

HONOR WHERE HONOR IS DUE

Here is another thought to consider: How can you celebrate your loved one? What can you do to express gratitude for the impact he or she made in your life?

I have officiated many funerals and have grown familiar with a phrase known as "tombstone testimonies." It refers to tombstone inscriptions that describe a loved one. It refers to the sentiments expressed about a loved one during the eulogy, over the casket, or at the burial site.

Another term you may have heard is "the dash," which refers to how someone lived their life from the date of birth to the date of death. It is not necessarily about the duration of one's life (number of years) but their donation of life—the contributions they made that can live on beyond their lifetime. That may be a sobering consideration for those of us who are still alive.

Wouldn't it be beneficial to our process if we spent time thinking about how we can celebrate our loved ones' lives? Could that possibly be a deterrent to excessive grieving? As difficult as it may seem, it may help to celebrate the good times shared. It may help to express gratefulness and love. It may help to express forgiveness toward those who may have caused harm.

So, how can you celebrate your loved one, whether that be today, tomorrow, or for as long as you live? Well, you can continue to use their name in conversations like, "My husband (insert name) and I loved that movie." "My sister (insert name) and I loved to travel." You may express the fact that your mom used to love to go on walks in the morning. It could be sharing the history, accomplishments, or achievements of your loved one with family or friends. It could be finishing a project that was left undone or fulfilling a dream they often talked about. It could be as simple as planting a tree or naming a child after your loved one. It may involve the entire family coming together and mutually contributing toward an idea. It may include an endowment fund in your loved one's name. These are just a few ideas that may help the recovery process. The options are at your discretion.

THE LITTLE FOXES

Every time someone or something of significance exits our lives, there may be sorrow. Whether it be the end of a job, career, contract, or a child leaving for college or getting married, we experience sadness. It can be felt when you are no longer able to do something you love, such as leaving a church family or moving to a new home or community, and some goodbyes are harder than others.

Why am I talking about this? I think we can easily identify the grief experienced due to the loss of life but often ignore the lesser departures, transitions, or changes that take place in our lives. Although they may be less significant, they carry weight.

When love, friendship, and associations become a part of our lives, and fond memories develop, a bond is made. However, when sadness or heartache develops as a result of a disconnect, we can mourn what was.

I encourage you to take a moment to reflect, focus your breathing, and laugh or cry if you feel the need. However, do not remain in a state of sorrow, but learn to appreciate and celebrate your experiences.

Release the sadness and be renewed so that grief does not grow and become something greater that subtly and adversely affects you. In Song of Solomon 2:15, it speaks of "The little foxes that spoil the vines."

Recognize the significant as well as the lesser forms of grief, and invite God into both to bring healing and wholeness into your life. Jesus said in John 10:10 (NLT), "...My purpose is to give them a rich and satisfying life."

Chrysanthemums symbolize truth, loyalty, and honesty.

PRAYER

Father, you know everything about me and what I have been through. I have tried to recover from grief but cannot seem to get better. Grief is wrecking my life.

Father, in the name of Jesus, I release my mourning, my grieving, my sadness today, that which has been prolonged. Father, whether I'm stuck in a season or a moment, I release it to You now so that I can move forward. I know that my life is not over.

In the name of Jesus, I pray that undue grief and the spirit of heaviness be lifted off of me. Like chains that have bound me, may they be shaken off, in the name of Jesus. Impart in me new dreams and new visions, God, so that I can move forward from the place of sackcloth and ashes.

Father, may I grab hold of Your hand, and may You walk me through this valley of the shadow of death and bring me to the other side. You promised me joy, and You promised me peace. Today, I take off this sorrow and put on the garment of praise.

I take authority over the spirit of heaviness and command it to stop operating in my life. From this moment forward, spirit of heaviness, you are no longer welcomed. You are rebuked, cast out, and must go and never return. Today, I declare that I am set free and will begin to experience joy, laughter, peace, and hope in my life. Today, I am healed, delivered, rescued, and I will recover.

I will live to glorify you, God. I will walk in the calling you have placed upon my life. I thank You for healing my grieving heart. Thank You, Holy Spirit, for your guidance from this day forward.

In Jesus' name. Amen.

Inspirational Verses

"You are my refuge and my shield; I have put my hope in your word."
—Psalm 119:114 (NIV)

"Even though I walk through the darkest valley, I will fear no evil, for you are with me."
— Psalm 23:4 (NIV)

"You, who have shown me great and severe troubles, Shall revive me again, And bring me up again from the depths of the earth. You shall increase my greatness, And comfort me on every side."
— Psalm 71:20-21

"Then they cried out to the Lord in their trouble, And He saved them out of their distresses. He brought them out of darkness and the shadow of death And broke their chains in pieces."
— Psalm 107:13-14

"In my distress I cried to the Lord, And He heard me."
— Psalm 120:1

"Because he has set his love upon Me, therefore I will deliver him; I will set him on high, because he has known My name. He shall call upon Me, and I will answer him; I will be with him in trouble; I will deliver him and honor him."
— Psalm 91:14-15

"When my spirit was overwhelmed within me, Then You knew my path. In the way in which I walk."
— Psalm 142:3

"My flesh and my heart fail; But God is the strength of my heart and my portion forever."
— Psalm 73:26

"Unless the Lord had been my help, My soul would soon have settled in silence. If I say, "My foot slips," Your mercy, O Lord, will hold me up. In the multitude of my anxieties within me, Your comforts delight my soul."
— Psalm 94:17-19

"For I am convinced that neither death nor life, neither angels nor demons, neither the present nor the future, nor any powers, neither height nor depth, nor anything else in all creation, will be able to separate us from the love of God that is in Christ Jesus our Lord."
— Romans 8:38-39

"The Lord your God is with you, the Mighty Warrior who saves."
— Zephaniah 3:17 (NIV)

"I called on your name, Lord, from the depths of the pit. You heard my plea: "Do not close your ears to my cry for relief." You came near when I called you, and you said, 'Do not fear.'"
— Lamentations 3:55-57 (NIV)

www.ingramcontent.com/pod-product-compliance
Lightning Source LLC
LaVergne TN
LVHW051527070426
835507LV00023B/3353